THIS NOTEBOOK
BELONGS TO:

ERNEST CREATIVE DESIGNS

Copyright © 2019.
All right reserved. No part of this book or this book as a whole may be used,
reproduced, or transmitted in any form or means
without written permission from publisher.

LETTERS

A B C D E F G H I J
K L M N O P Q R S T U V
W X Y Z

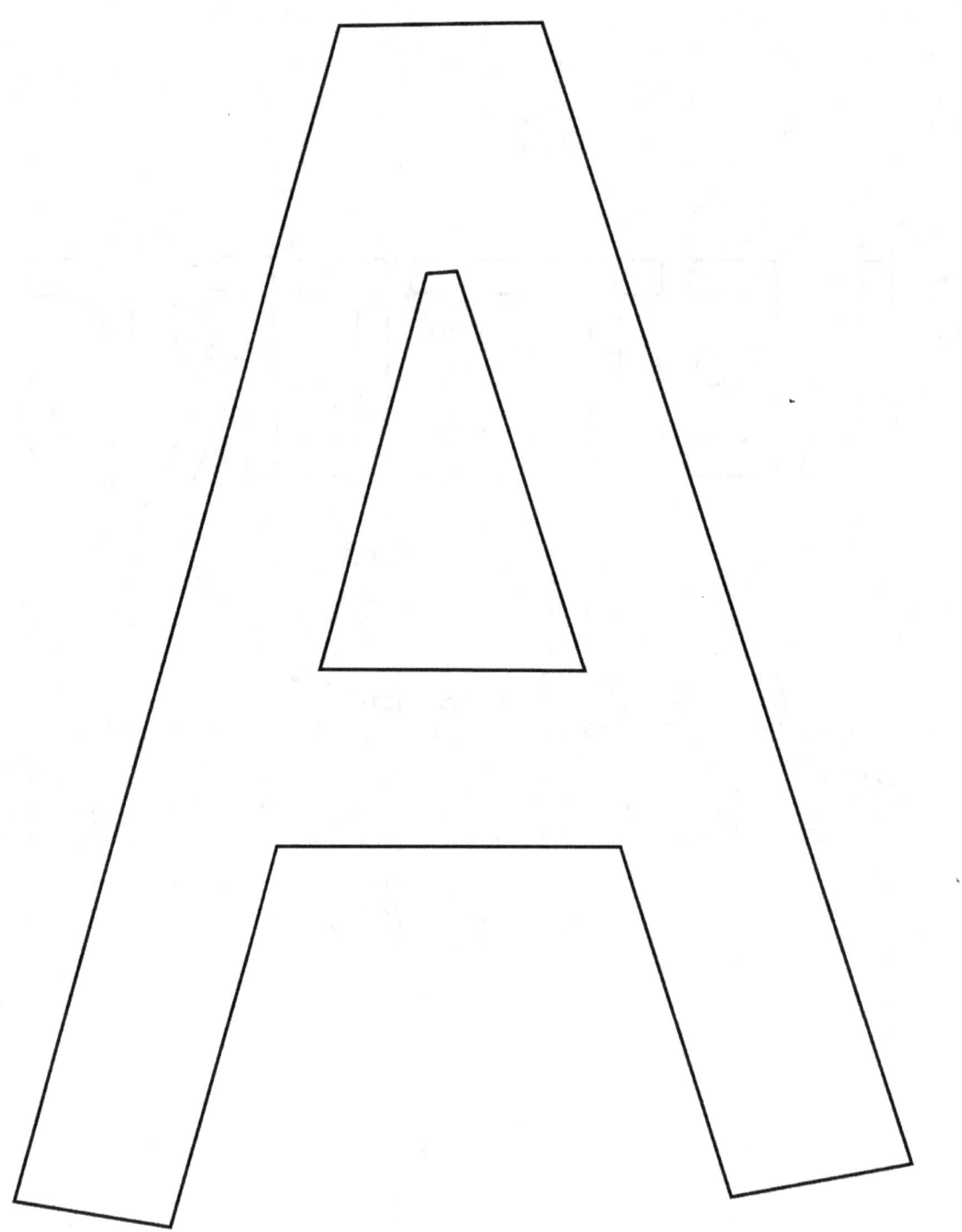

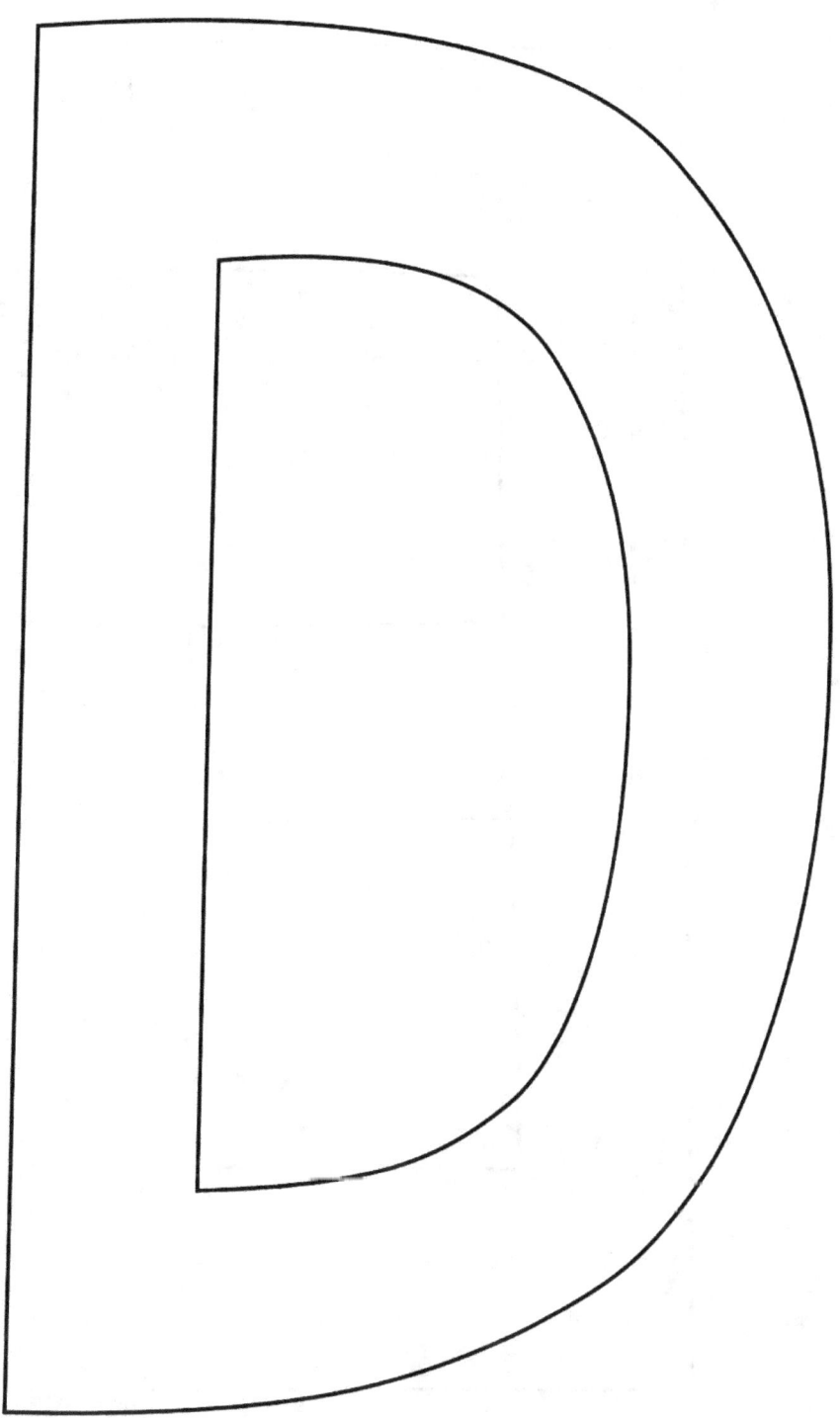

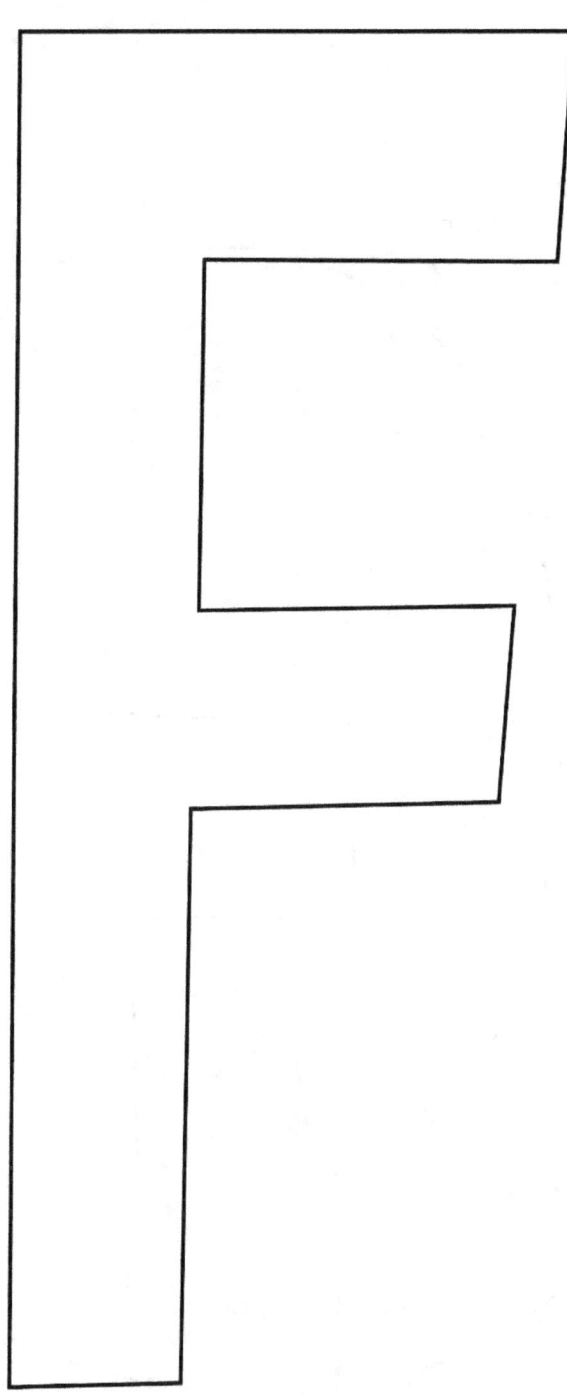

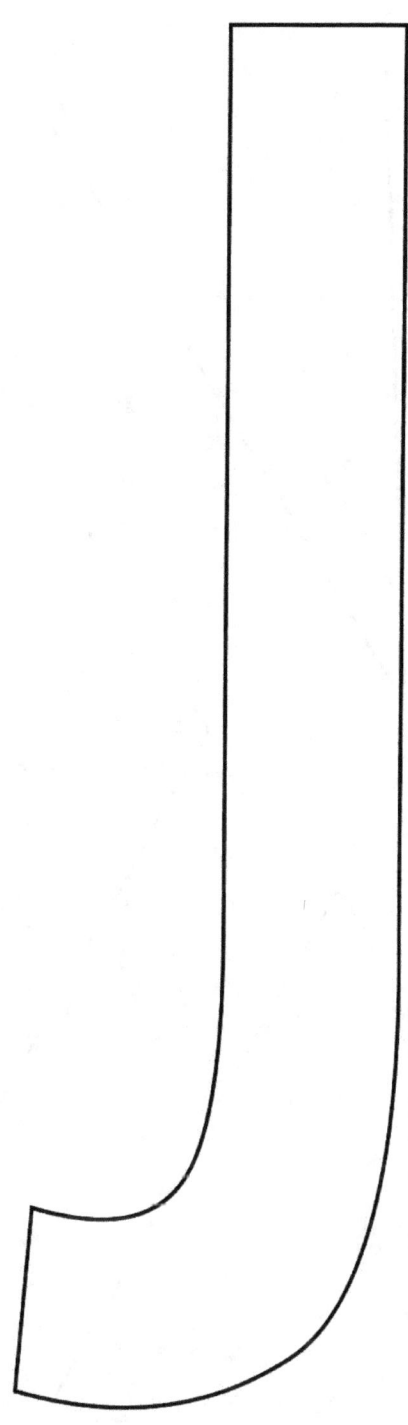

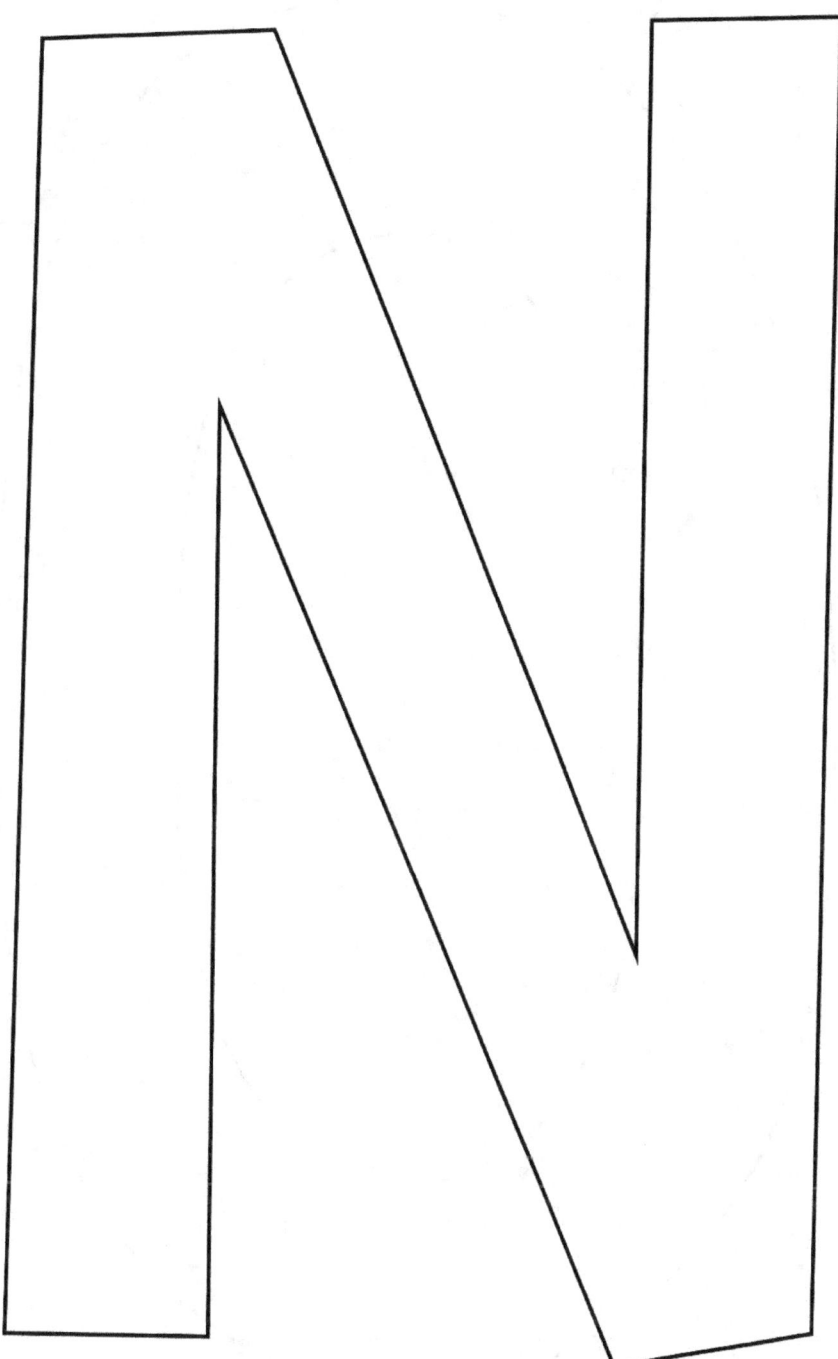

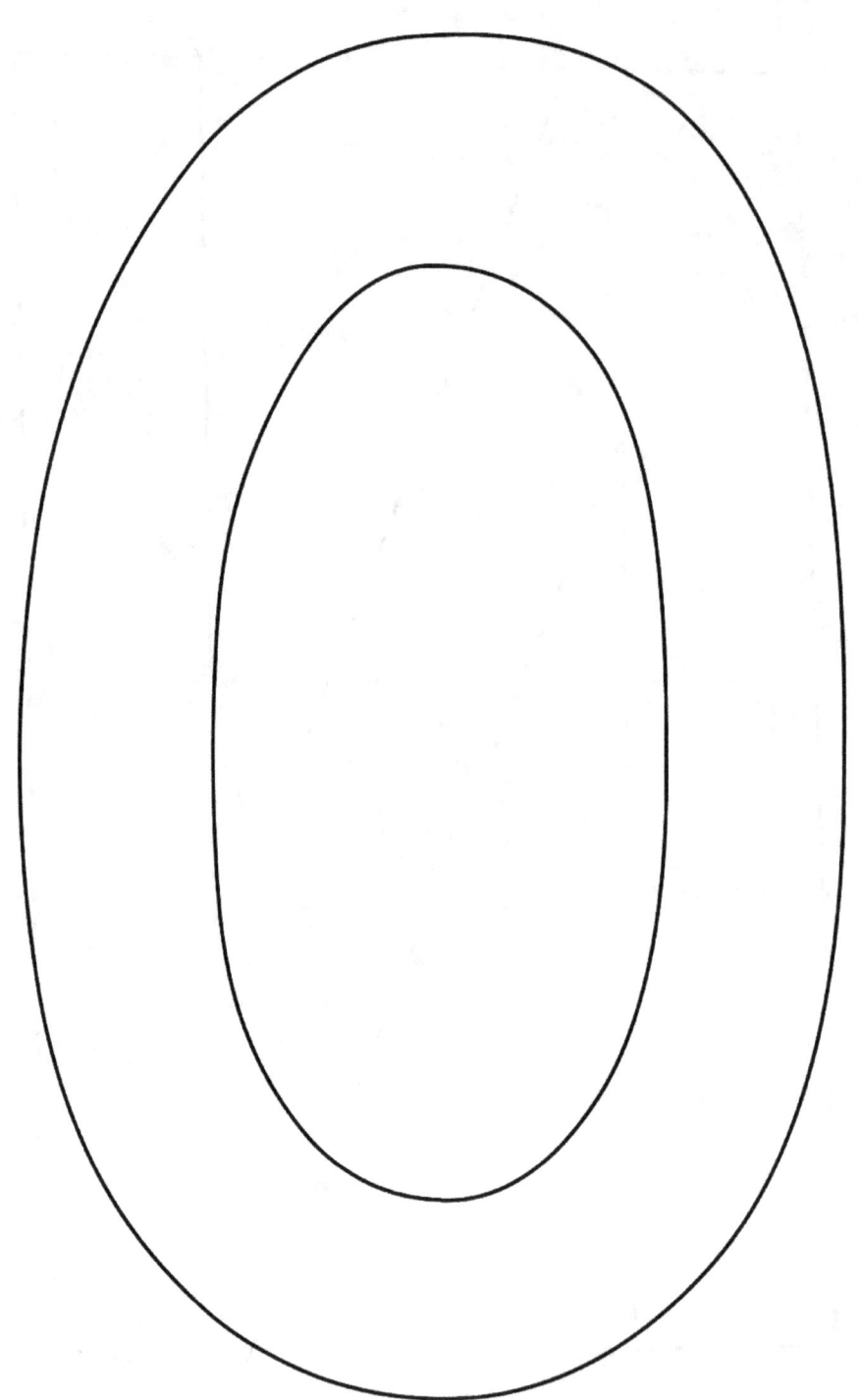

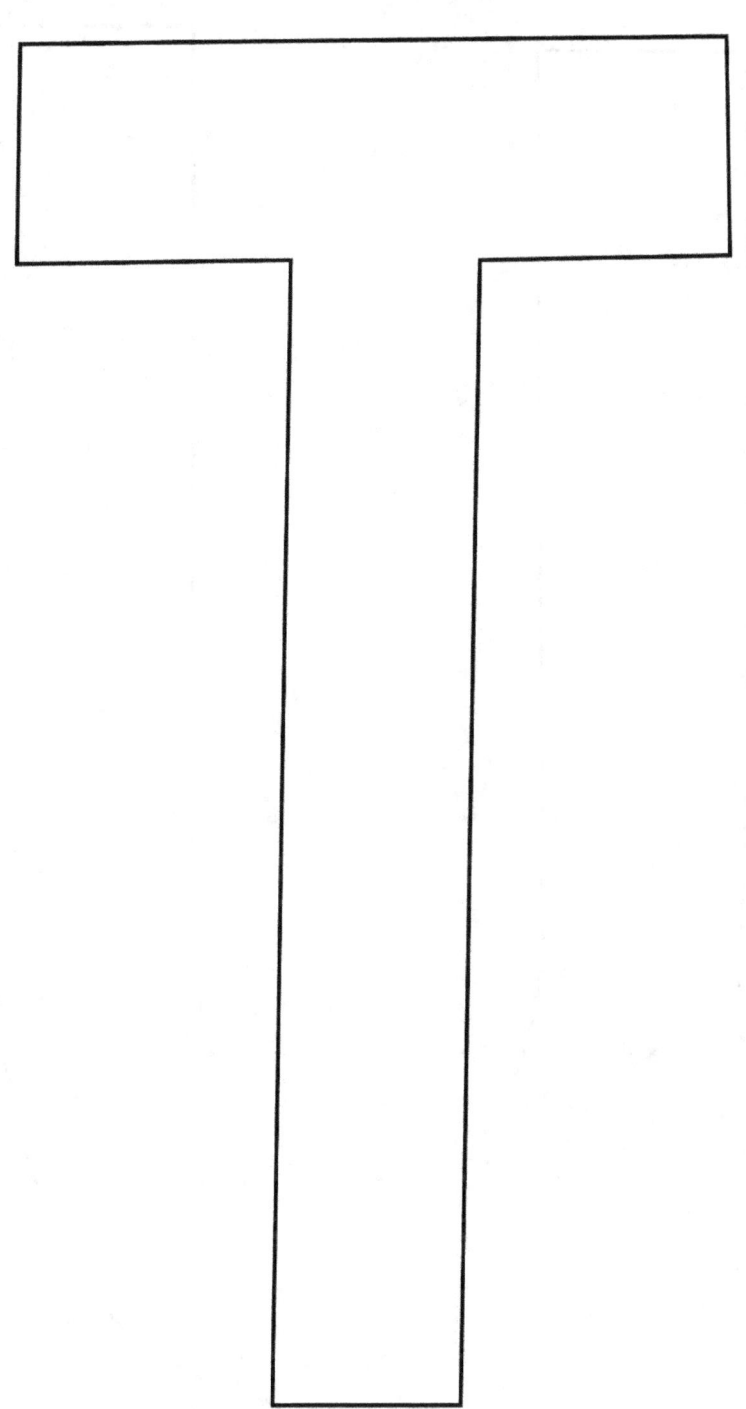

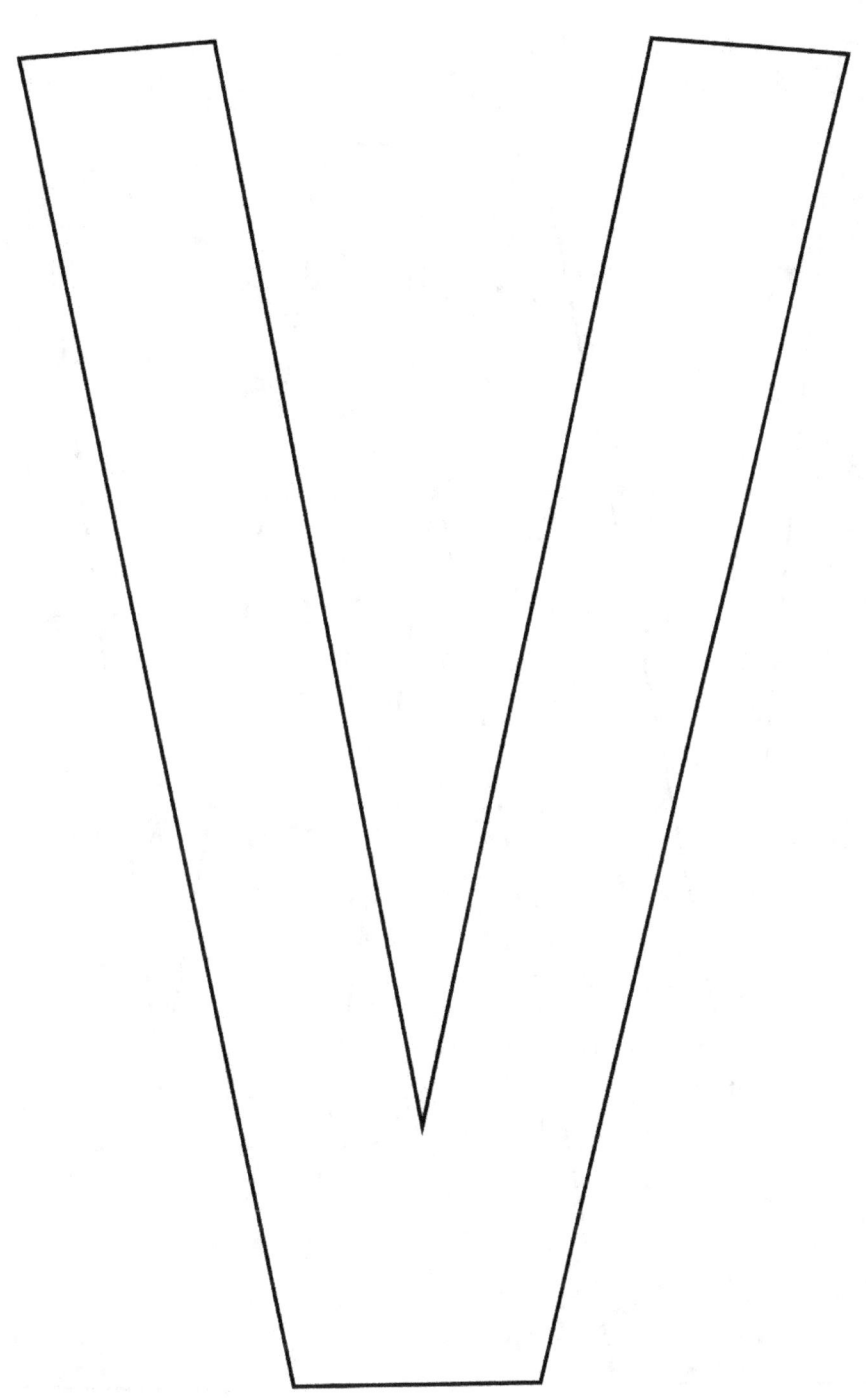

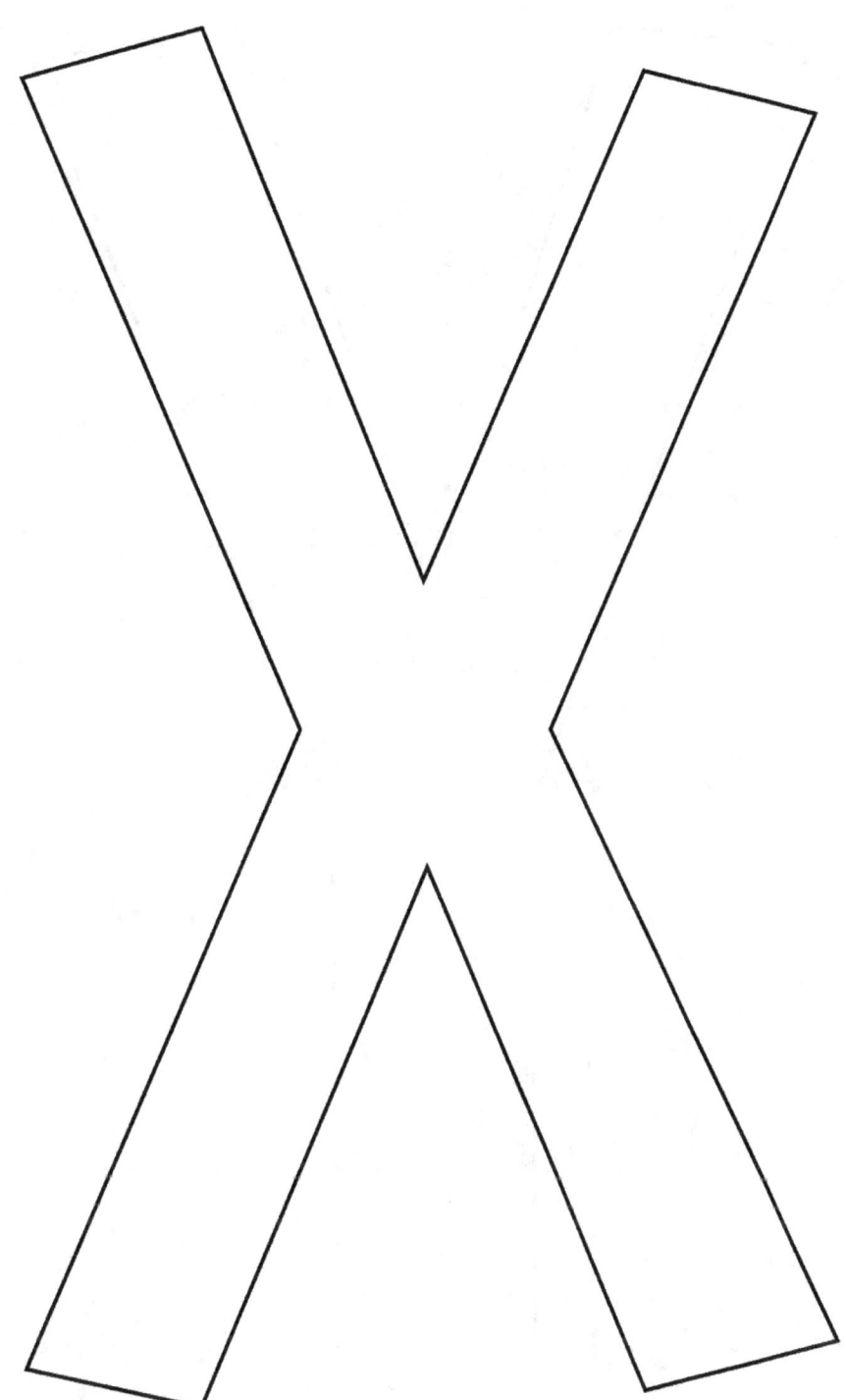

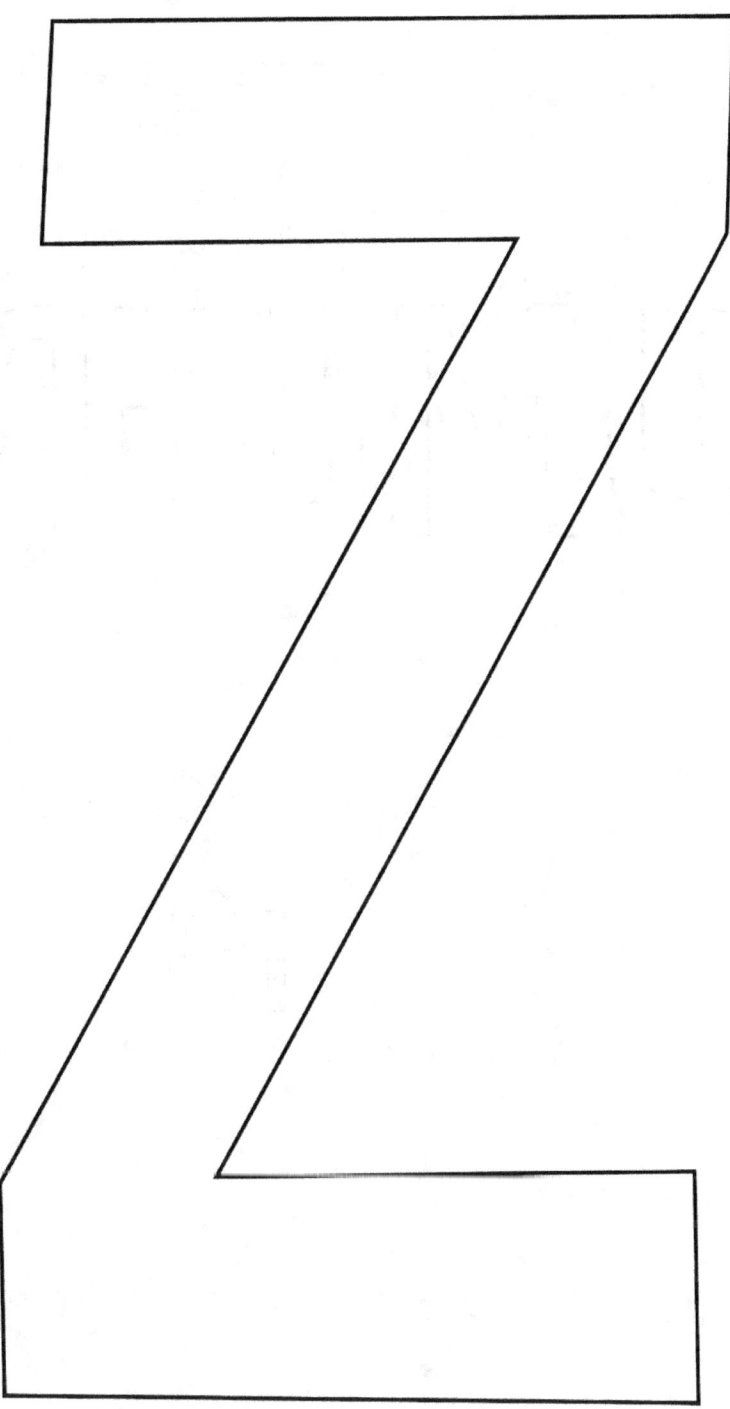

NUMBERS

0 1 2 3 4 5 6 7
8 9 10

0

ZERO

1

ONE

2

TWO

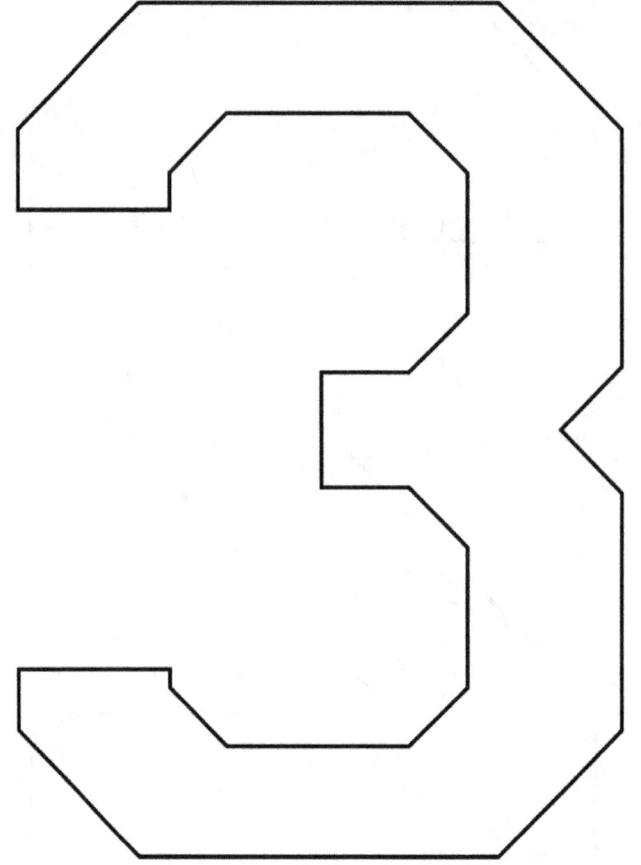

THREE

5

FIVE

6

SIX

7

SEVEN

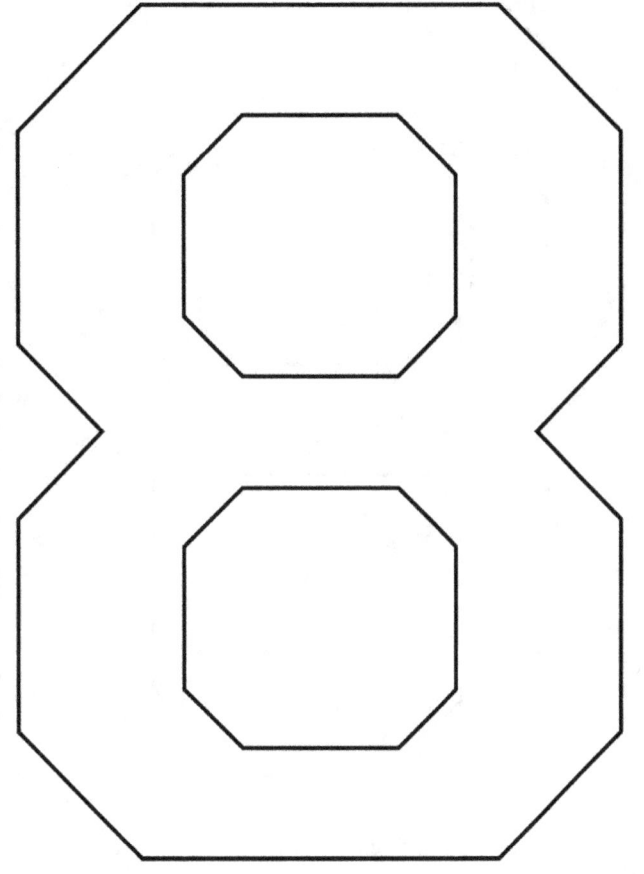

EIGHT

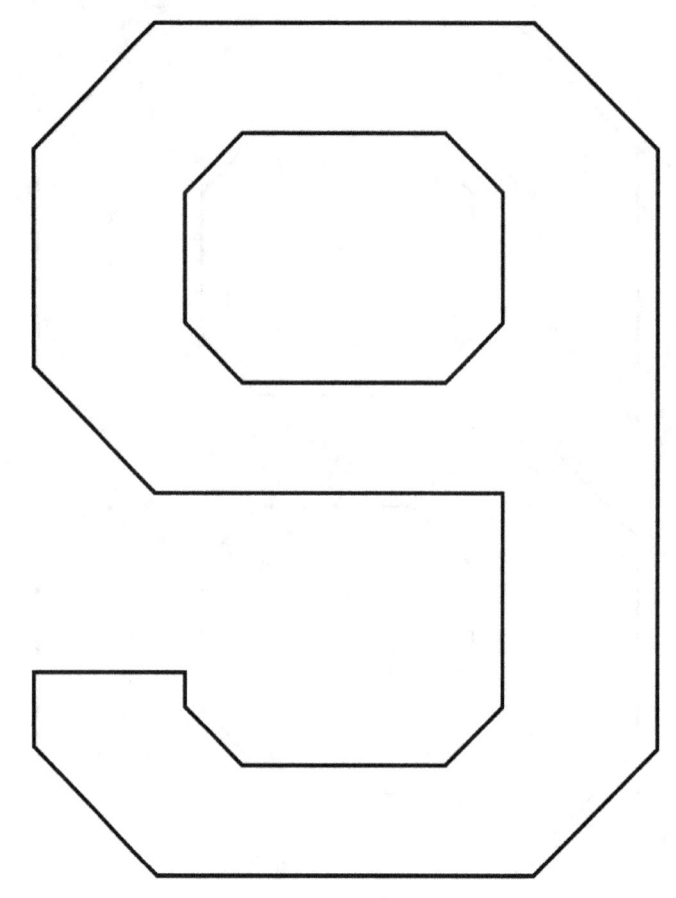

10

TEN

SHAPES

SQUARE

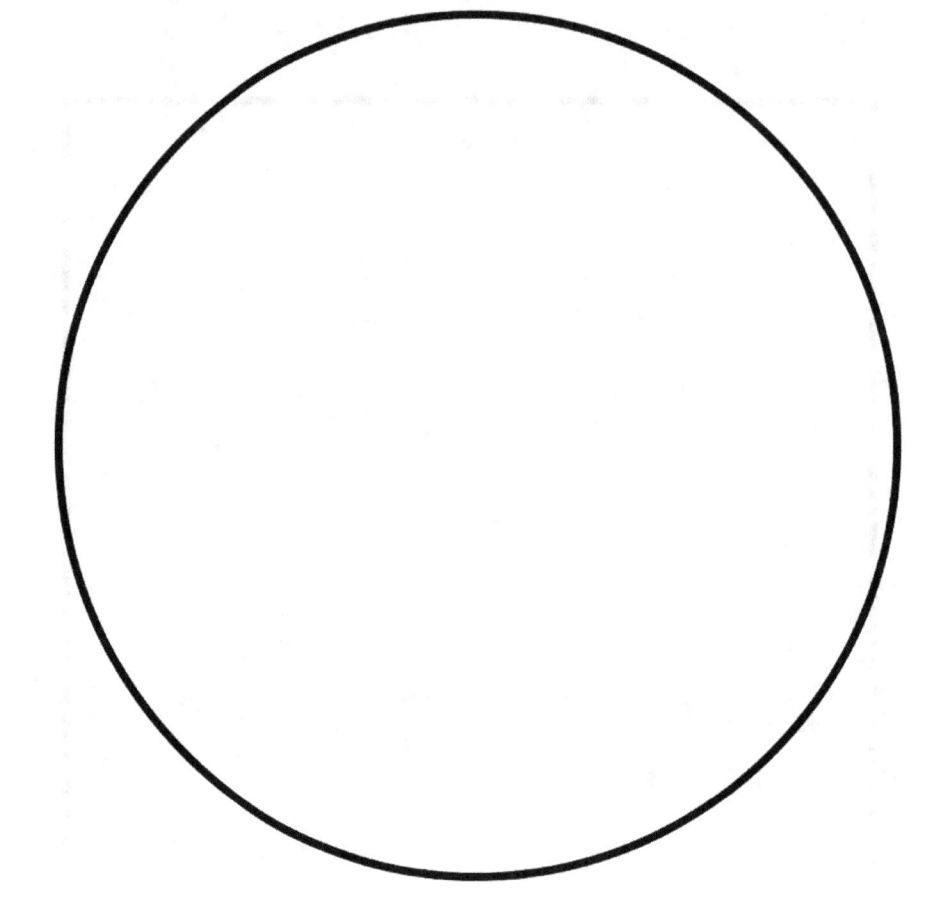

CIRCLE

HEART

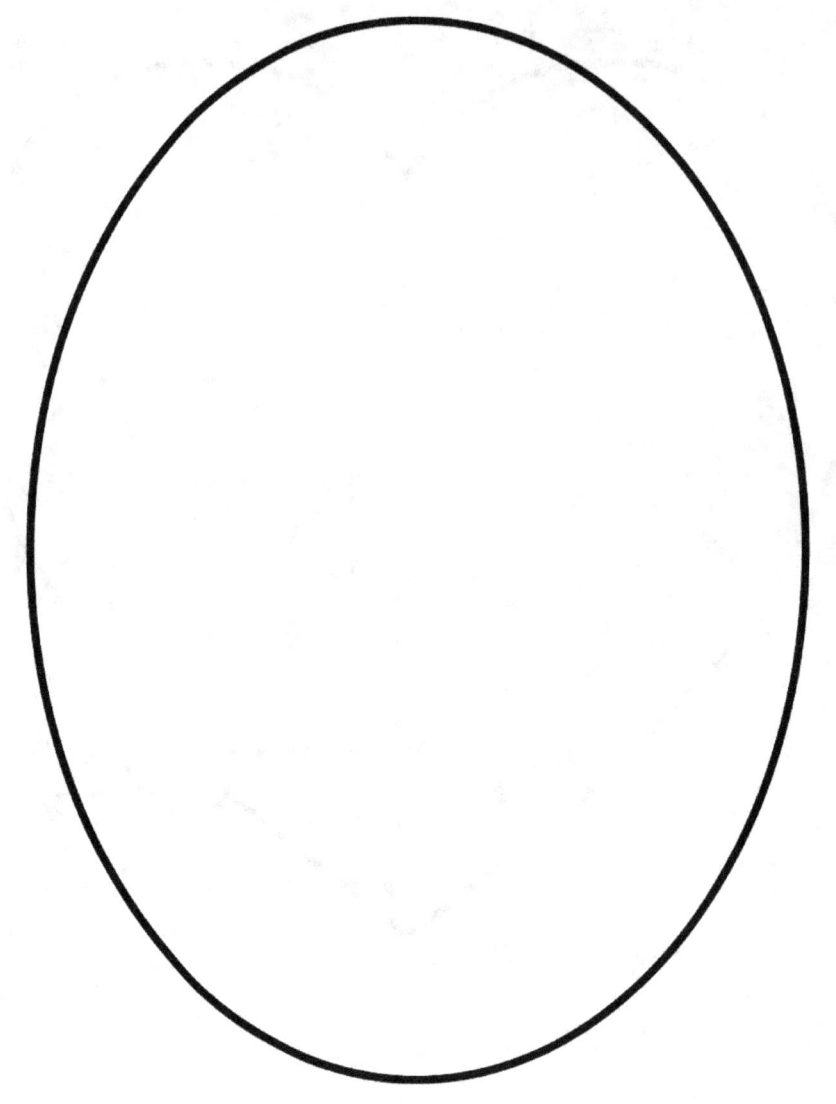

ELLIPSE

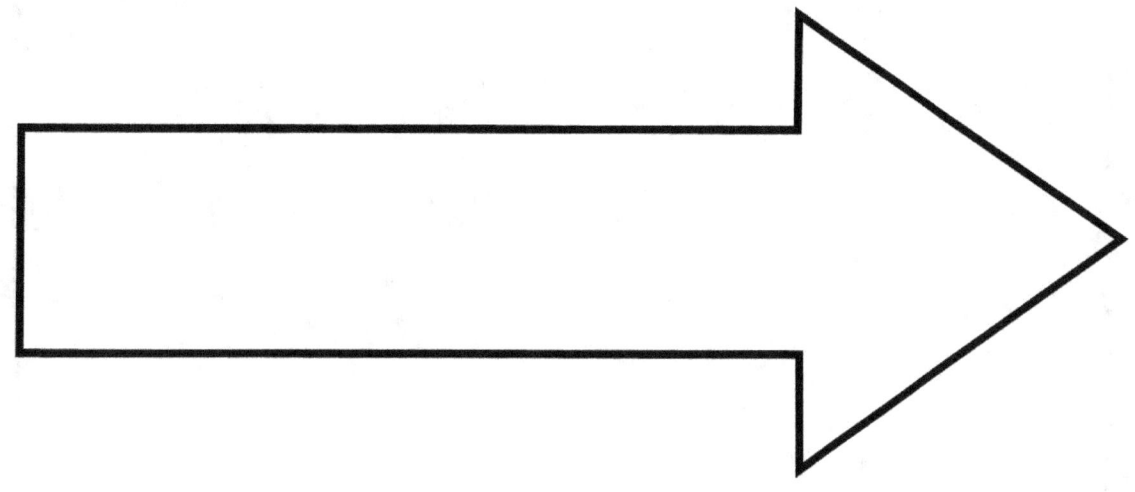

ARROW

RECTANGLE

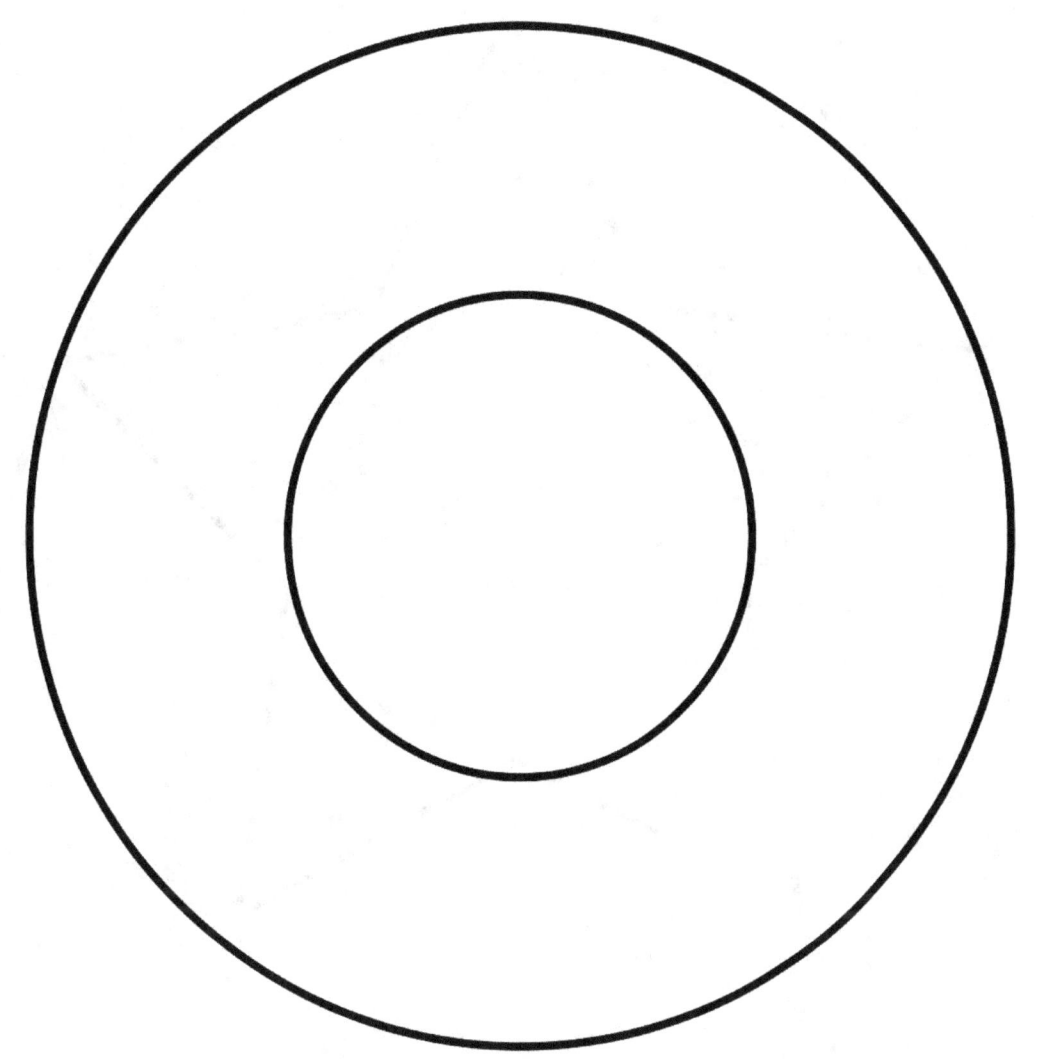

RINGE

STAR

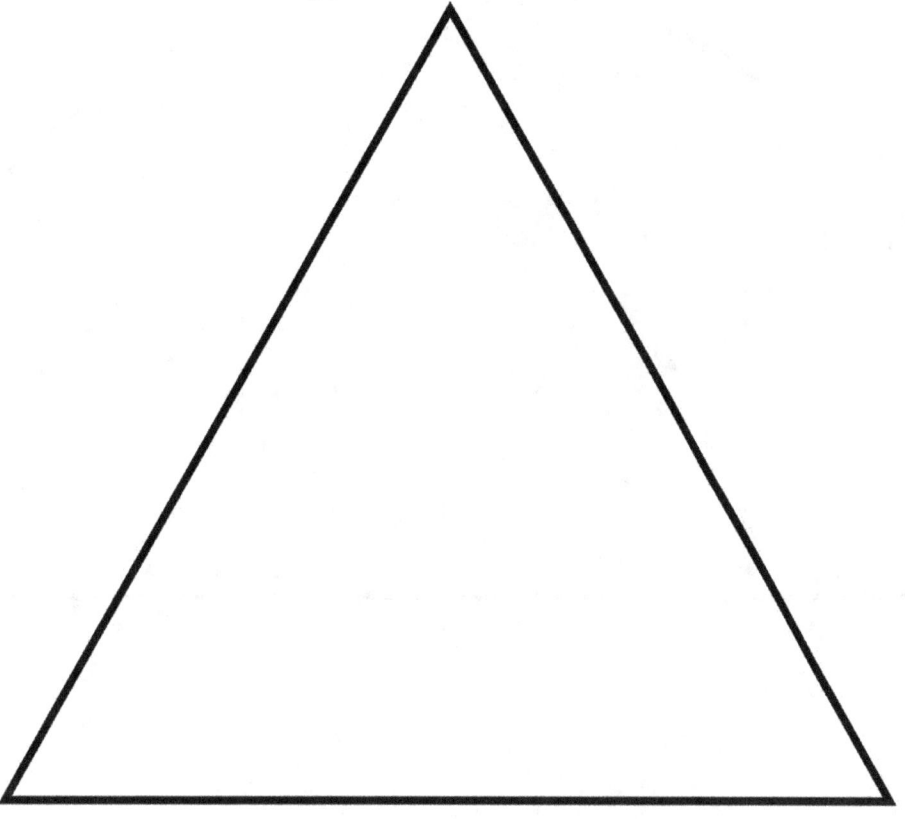

TRIANGLE

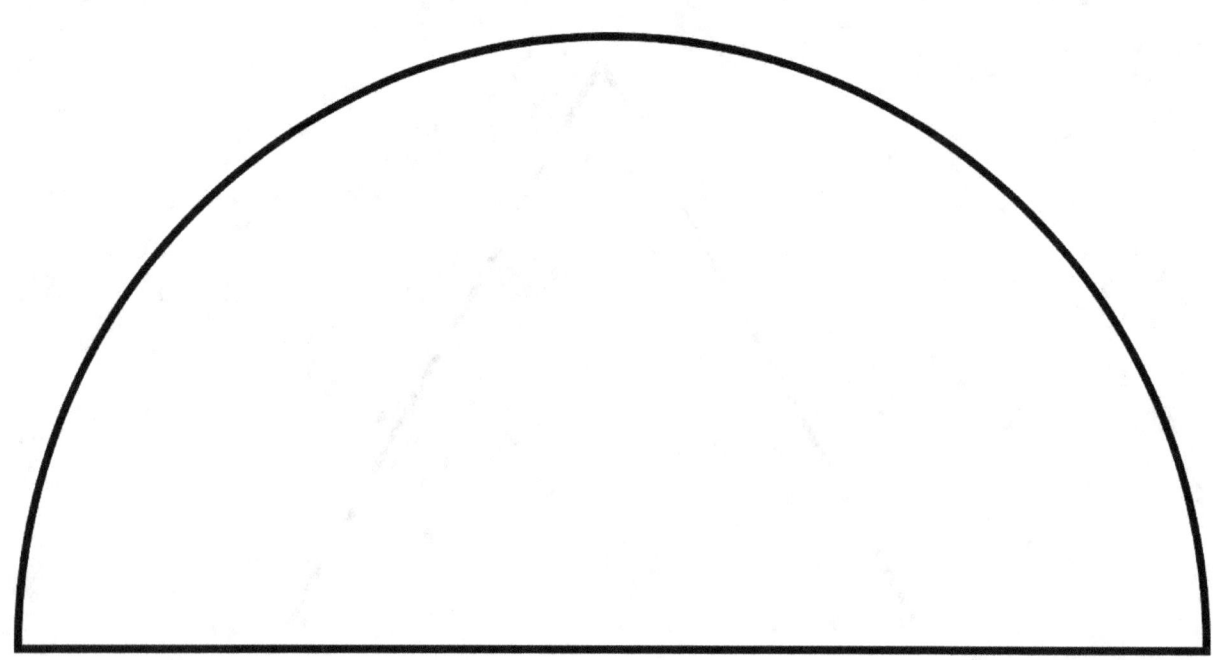

SEMICIRCLE

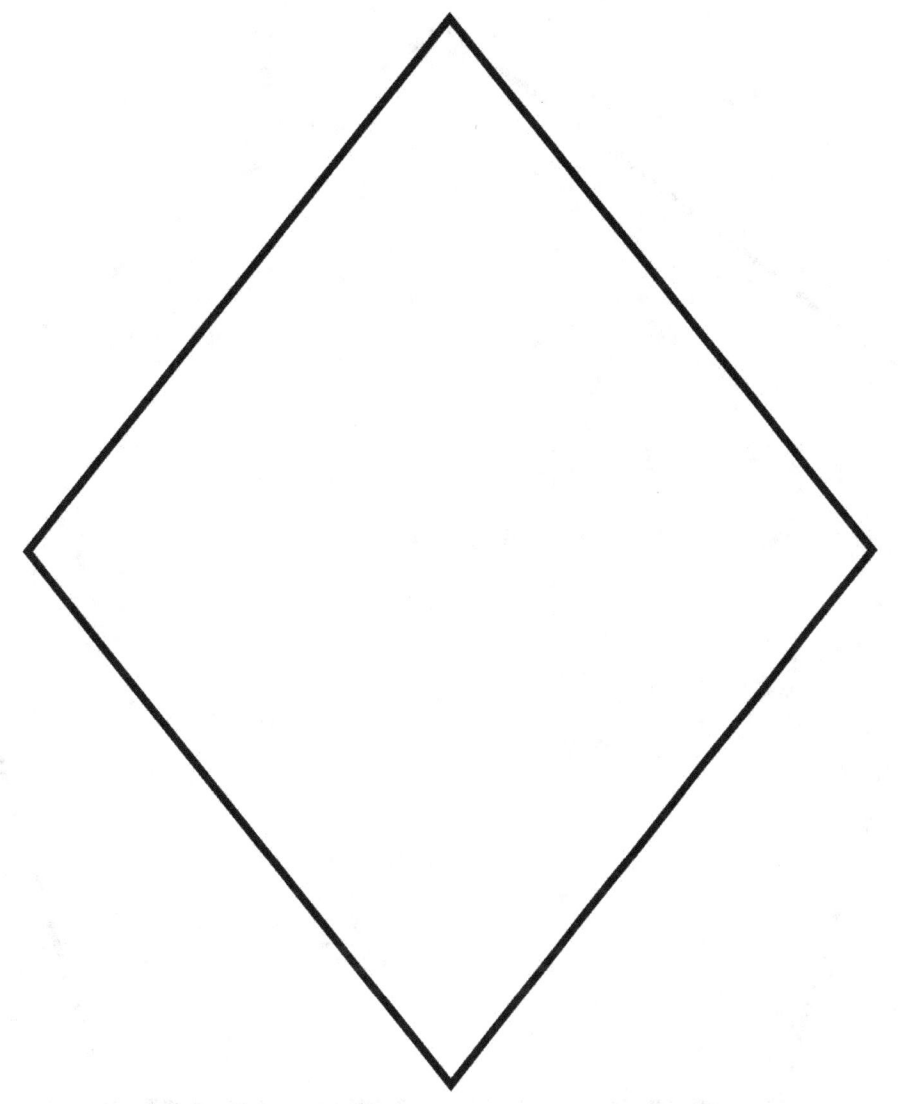

RHOMBUS

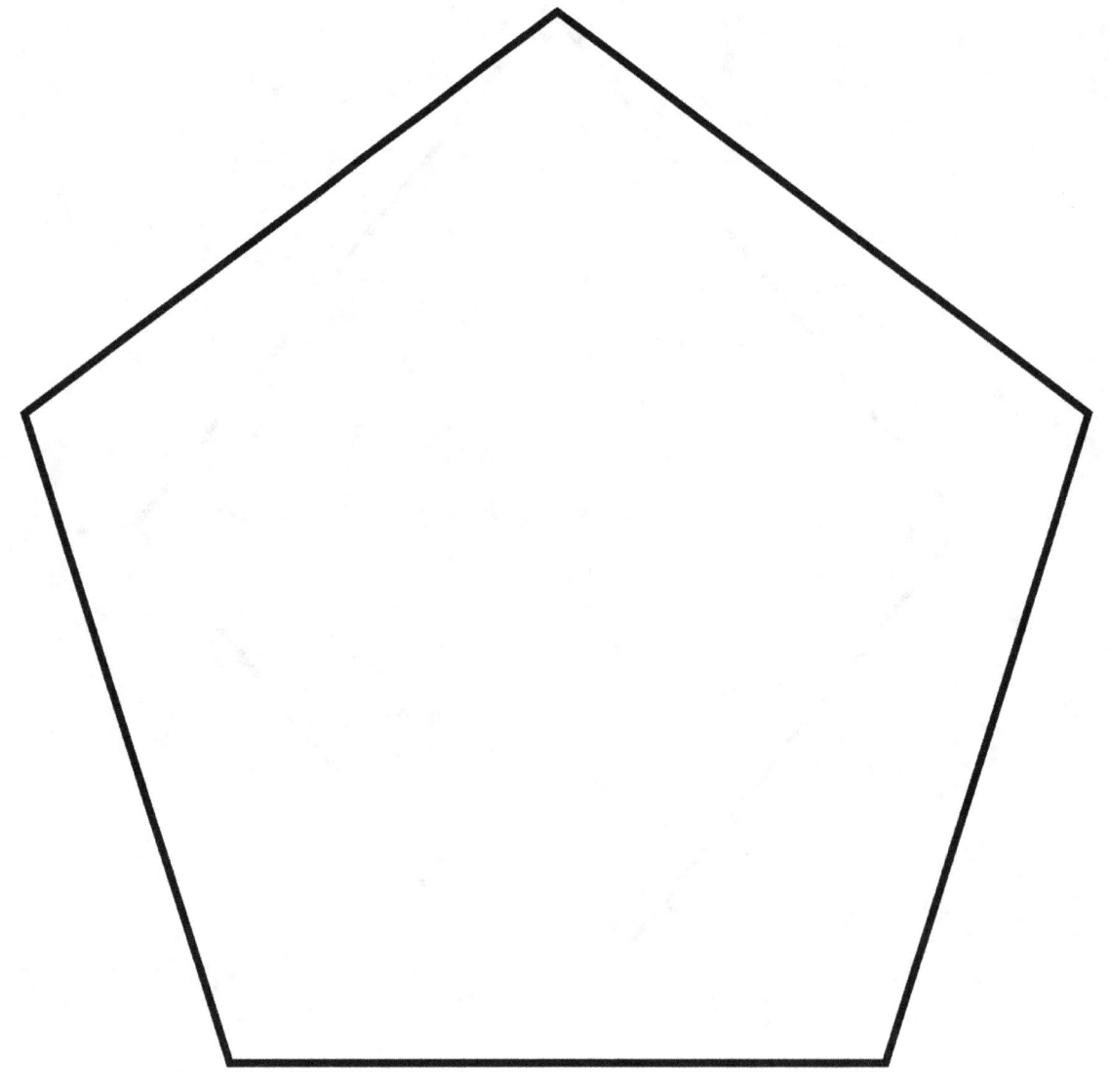

PENTAGON

ANIMALS

CAT

ELEPHANT

FOX

CHICKENS

ALLIGATOR

BEAR

MONKEY

PANDA

ZEBRA

FOOD

GARLIC

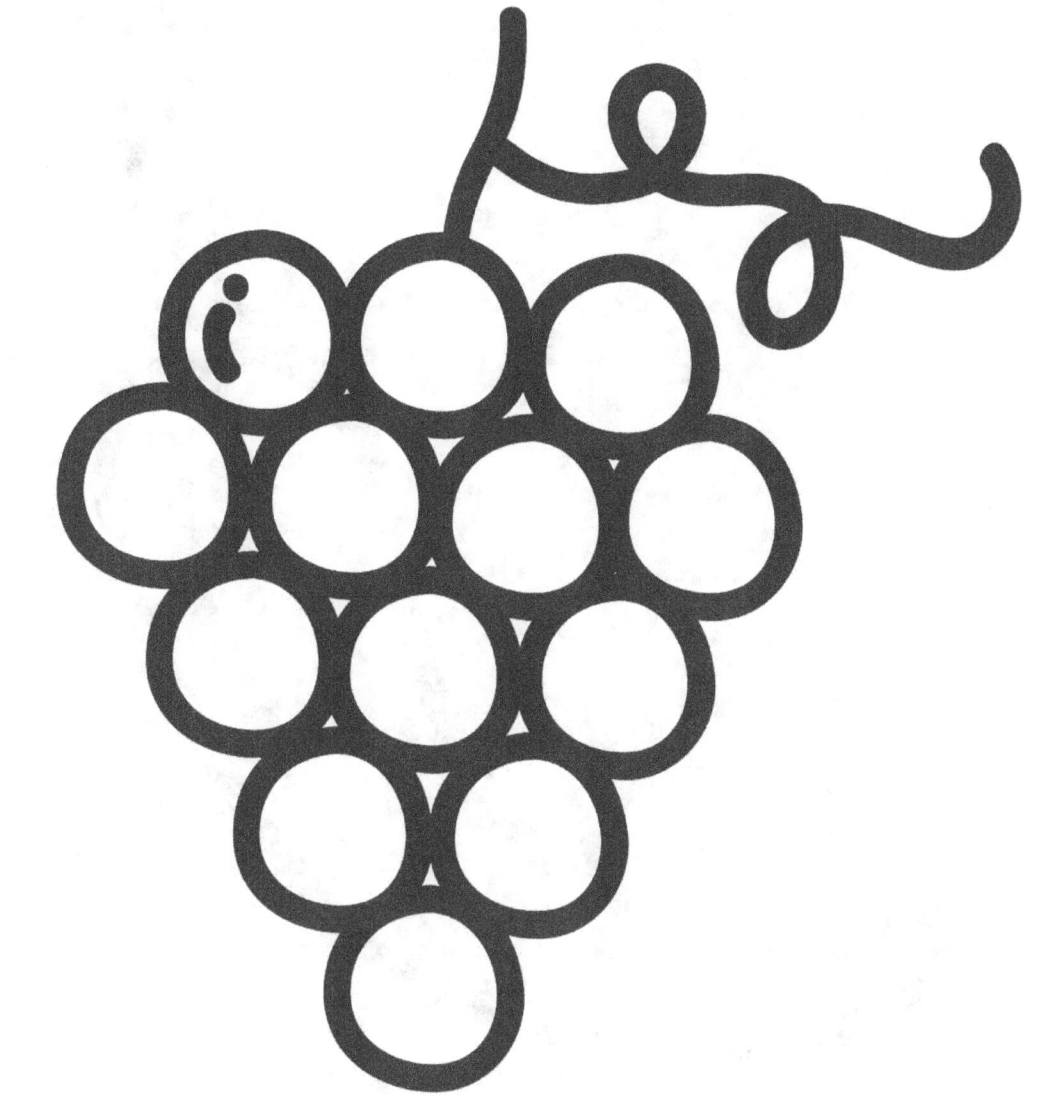

GRAPES

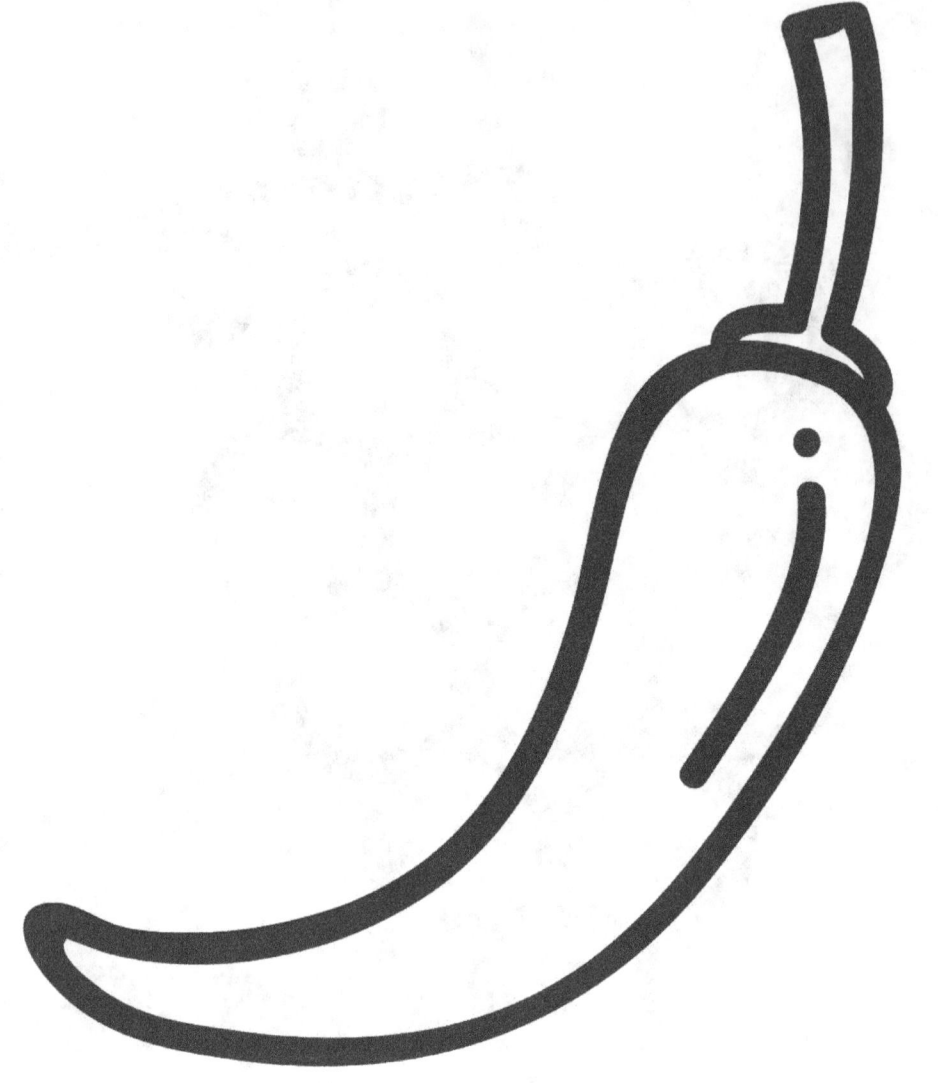

HOT PEPPER

LEMON

MASHROOMS

ONION

PEAR

PUMPKIN

STRAWBERRY

TANGERINE

TOMATO

WATERMELON

BANANA

CARROT

DRAWING SPACE

www.ingramcontent.com/pod-product-compliance
Lightning Source LLC
Chambersburg PA
CBHW081449220526
45466CB00008B/2567